BENSON INYANGALA

SERVANT LEADERSHIP FOR LOCAL CHURCH GROWTH AND SOCIETAL TRANSFORMATION

BENSON INYANGALA

SERVANT LEADERSHIP FOR LOCAL CHURCH GROWTH AND SOCIETAL TRANSFORMATION

SERVANT LEADERHIP AND TRANSFORMATION

Blessed Hope Publishing

Imprint

Any brand names and product names mentioned in this book are subject to trademark, brand or patent protection and are trademarks or registered trademarks of their respective holders. The use of brand names, product names, common names, trade names, product descriptions etc. even without a particular marking in this work is in no way to be construed to mean that such names may be regarded as unrestricted in respect of trademark and brand protection legislation and could thus be used by anyone.

Cover image: www.ingimage.com

Publisher:
Blessed Hope Publishing
is a trademark of
Dodo Books Indian Ocean Ltd. and OmniScriptum S.R.L publishing group

120 High Road, East Finchley, London, N2 9ED, United Kingdom
Str. Armeneasca 28/1, office 1, Chisinau MD-2012, Republic of Moldova, Europe

ISBN: 978-620-4-18863-8

Copyright © BENSON INYANGALA
Copyright © 2024 Dodo Books Indian Ocean Ltd. and OmniScriptum S.R.L publishing group

SERVANT LEADERSHIP FOR LOCAL CHURCH GROWTH AND SOCIETAL TRANSFORMATION

BENSON OTEMBA INYANGALA

November 2024

Introduction

In this publication the author will discuss the critical significance of servant leadership in the Church and society. The author will advance the position that leadership in church should emulate the model set by Jesus Christ himself. The paper begins with a brief definition of leadership and the functions of leadership. Then the author zeroes in on servant leadership and characteristics of effective Christian leaders. Christian discipleship is then discussed followed by church – state relations and church and politics. The author posits that leadership and church ministry ought to engage with the society for impact. Towards the end of this article, the author emphasizes the critical role trust plays in the life of the leader. Eight pillars of trust are then described.

Leadership is influence.[1] One of the keys to recognizing a leader is to recognize when the act of leadership (influence) is actually occurring.[2] A leadership act is the identifiable influence of a person or persons at a given time that changes the perception or behaviour of a group towards a goal. A leadership act has the following four components: an influencer (this may be one of several persons), the followers (a person or persons who are being influenced), influence (the behaviour, and perception which brings about change) and a change (the different way of

---

[1] John C. Maxwell. *The 21 Irrefutable Laws of Leadership: Follow them and people will follow you*, Harper Collins Leadership, 1998, p. 13

[2] J. Robert Clinton. *The making of a leader*. Navpress. 1988, p.127

perceiving and behaving by the group). A leadership act occurs when someone has momentary influence over the group or situation.

A leader is identified as one who consistently performs leadership acts. The emergence of vision and the ongoing, consistent performance of leadership acts that help accomplish that vision are keys to distinguishing a leader from one who sometimes exercises influence over a group. After studying more than 700 Christian leaders, from biblical times to the present era, Dr. J. Robert Clinton coined the definition: A leader is a person with God-given capacity, and a God-given responsibility, who is influencing a specific group of God's people, toward God's purposes for that group.

"God-given capacity" refers to one's spiritual giftedness, natural abilities and acquired skills. "God-given responsibility" refers to a sense of accountability to God for the burden (call) he gives a leader for influencing others, and how and where the leader leads the people of God. "Influence" refers to the capacity to affect others and alter or change their thoughts or behaviour. It is persuasion backed by credibility. In our information society, leadership is influence. Whoever has the influence has the leadership, regardless of his position. "God's people" remind the leader that the church and its people belong to the Lord. He is the Chief Shepherd. "God's purposes" refer to those unique callings and biblical mandates that God gives his people. They are the commands of scripture, are ageless in their call, but have been uniquely applied in each generation.

Leadership functions

Leadership functions describe what all leaders must do or be responsible for as they influence their followers toward God' purposes. Leadership functions help one recognize and identify the essentials of a leader. A leader's actions and ministry include: "Relational functions" – related to the specific group of people God has given a leader to lead. They include team, ministry environment, care, feeding and development. "Task functions" – related to a leader's ministry assignment and group goals. These include organization, structures, decisions, finances and administration. "Visionary function" – related to hearing God and setting ministry direction. Included are issues of motivation, ownership, priorities and change.

Leaders often carry out these three functions simultaneously. The functions can vary, depending on the demands of a leader's current ministry assignment. The specific leadership functions below help further identify the characteristics and responsibilities of a leader. "Model" – they live out their vision in actions and lifestyle. Motivate – they inspire so others can follow. "Encourage" – they come alongside to exhort and admonish. "Facilitate" – they empower others, helping them excel. "Coordinate" – they bring people together. "Responsible" – they are willing to be accountable. "Develop" – they are conscious of the need for personal growth.

"Problem solving" – they can recognize and solve critical issues. "Decision making" – they can make necessary decisions. "Crisis resolution" – they acquire resources for emergency needs. "Apprentice" – they constantly seek to train new leaders.

Leadership style refers to the blend of a leader's personality, temperament and shaping. Style reflects the preferences and roles leaders are most equipped to fulfil. By identifying leadership style, leaders can better understand their unique fit in the ministry, and they can learn to value others' roles and contributions. Ministry conflicts often occur because leaders do not understand or value other styles of leadership. Many tests help define leadership styles. Personality Profile (Sanguine, Choleric, Melancholy, Phlegmatic), DISC = D- Dominant, I-Influencer, S-Steady, C-Compliant), Myers-Briggs, etc. Most tests reveal four basic styles. Creator, Developer, Maximizer, Redeveloper. Though no one style perfectly describes anyone, the groupings are helpful. Most leaders are a combination of these four styles.

Servant Leadership

The term "servant leader" was coined by Greenleaf. In 1977, Robert Greenleaf, then an executive in the communications industry, announced to the world that a new moral principle was emerging in society. He wrote that in the future, "the only truly viable institutions will be those that are predominantly servant-led.[3]

According to Dr Thorsten Grahn it is the focus on the growth of the individual, that they might flourish and achieve their full potential and not primarily the growth and potential of the organization that distinguishes servant leadership from other leadership styles.[4] The primary concern of the servant leader is service to their followers. From the teaching and example of Jesus Christ we learn that being a servant leader in the most general sense means being:

- A **voluntary** servant, who submits themselves to a higher purpose, which is beyond their personal interests or the interests of others,
- A **leader** who uses the power that is entrusted to them to serve others,
- A **servant** who, out of love, serves others needs before their own,
- A **teacher** who teaches their followers, in word and deed, how to become servant leaders themselves.

Applying these considerations of Jesus as a role model for Christian leaders we can see that, from a Biblical perspective, a servant leader is a person, who is:

- **Christ-centered** in all aspects of life (a voluntary servant of Christ)

---

[3] Robert K. Greenleaf. *Servant Leadership: a journey into the nature of legitimate power and greatness*. Paulistic Press:New Jersey, 1977, p.10.
[4] Thorsten Grahn. The Three Sisters Garden Analogy for Servant Leadership Based Collaboration. *The Journal of Virtues & Leadership*, Vol.2 Iss.1, Summer 2011, p.1-5.

- **Committed to serve** the needs of others before their own,
- **Courageous to lead** with power and love as an expression of serving,
- **Consistently developing** others into servant leaders, and
- **Continually inviting feedback** from those that they want to serve in order to grow towards the ultimate servant leader, Jesus Christ.

Robert Greenleaf identified the following qualities of a servant leader:

1. **Listening** - Traditionally, leaders have been valued for their communication and decision making skills. Servant-leaders must reinforce these important skills by making a deep commitment to listening intently to others. Servant-leaders seek to identify and clarify the will of a group. They seek to listen receptively to what is being said (and not said). Listening also encompasses getting in touch with one's inner voice, and seeking to understand what one's body, spirit, and mind are communicating.

2. **Empathy** - Servant-leaders strive to understand and empathize with others. People need to be accepted and recognized for their special and unique spirit. One must assume the good intentions of coworkers and not reject them as people, even when forced to reject their behavior or performance.

3. **Healing** - Learning to heal is a powerful force for transformation and integration. One of the great strengths of servant-leadership is the potential for healing one's self and others. In "The Servant as Leader", Greenleaf

writes, "There is something subtle communicated to one who is being served and led if, implicit in the compact between the servant-leader and led is the understanding that the search for wholeness is something that they have."

4. **Awareness** - General awareness, and especially self-awareness, strengthens the servant-leader. Making a commitment to foster awareness can be scary-- one never knows that one may discover! As Greenleaf observed, "Awareness is not a giver of solace - it's just the opposite. It disturbed. They are not seekers of solace. They have their own inner security."

5. **Persuasion** - Servant-leaders rely on persuasion, rather than positional authority in making decisions. Servant-leaders seek to convince others, rather than coerce compliance. This particular element offers one of the clearest distinctions between the traditional authoritarian model and that of servant-leadership. The servant-leader is effective at building consensus within groups.

6. **Conceptualization** - Servant-leaders seek to nurture their abilities to "dream great dreams." The ability to look at a problem (or an organization) from a conceptualizing perspective means that one must think beyond day-to-day realities. Servant-leaders must seek a delicate balance between conceptualization and day-to-day focus.

7. **Foresight** - Foresight is a characteristic that enables servant-leaders to understand lessons from the past, the realities of the present, and the likely

consequence of a decision in the future. It is deeply rooted in the intuitive mind.

8. **Stewardship** - Robert Greenleaf's view of all institutions was one in which CEO's, staff, directors, and trustees all play significance roles in holding their institutions in trust for the great good of society.

9. **Commitment to the Growth of People** - Servant-leaders believe that people have an intrinsic value beyond their tangible contributions as workers. As such, servant-leaders are deeply committed to a personal, professional, and spiritual growth of each and every individual within the organization.

10. **Building Community** - Servant-leaders are aware that the shift from local communities to large institutions as the primary shaper of human lives has changed our perceptions and has caused a feeling of loss. Servant-leaders seek to identify a means for building community among those who work within a given institution.

Effective Christian Leaders

Firstly, effective Christian leaders possess a God-given vision and are passionate about it. A God-given vision is what drives leaders and churches. Without one, the leader lacks purpose and a direction in which to lead. Vision, furthermore, goes beyond the leader just possessing the vision. Once the effective leader has the vision, he or she passionately casts that vision to co-leaders and followers. Casting vision is important because, as Andy Stanley writes, it "clarifies the win."[5] What is meant by that statement is that everyone is on the same page; from co-leaders to followers. Everyone understands what the church is about, can comprehend what the vision and mission of the church are, and understands how the church is working to fulfill its mission and vision. Through possessing and casting a God-given vision, leaders can fulfill in their churches, the wishes that Paul had for the Thessalonian church when he wrote to them, "May the Lord direct your hearts into God's love and Christ's perseverance," (1 Thessalonians 3:5 – NIV).

Secondly, effective Christian leaders possess the ability to properly live in the dialectical tension between maintaining structure and allowing for change and creativity. Narrowly focused and overly structured leaders stifle creativity. Maintaining the status quo is not always the best way of leading. Ideally, the effective Christian leader will allow for creative ideas to improve upon existing ministries in the church, and for creative solutions to problems.

The idea that there is only one way to do something is counterproductive to effective Christian leadership. One must keep in mind, however, that on the other side of this dialectical tension is the need to maintain some sort of structure. In allowing for creativity, the leader should want to keep some standards that keep the church or organization true to the God-given vision that it has. I agree with Tim Keel when he suggests that leaders should consider taking a posture of surrender. In

---

[5] Andy Stanley, Reggie Joiner, and Lane Jones. *7 Practices of Effective Ministry*. Colorado Springs: Multnomah Books, 2004, 75.

doing so leaders surrender some of their control in order to stay present in what he calls chaos, just long enough to be able to discern the work the Holy Spirit wants to do in love and creativity over a "new act of creation." Keel writes that this is not "a posture of control but of balance, awareness and adjustment."[6] Effective leaders live in proper dialectical tension between maintaining structure (control) and being open to creativity and change (chaos).

The third thing that makes an effective Christian leader is the ability to avoid certain temptations that every Christian leader is bound to face. In his book, "In the name of Jesus" Henri Nouwen says that there are three temptations in particular that afflict every Christian leader; the temptations to be relevant, spectacular and powerful.[7] I would agree with Nouwen that these are very powerful and common temptations that leaders face.

Christian leaders must resist the temptation to compromise their values and their vision for the purpose of being relevant. Leaders will face the temptation to want to be the leader of the cool, relevant church that attracts people through "hip" music or catchy topical sermon series. When leaders give into this temptation they face the danger of watering down the gospel, and miss the point of Jesus' Great Commission in Matthew 28 – to make disciples. Of course, everyone wants to be

---

[6] Tim Keel. *Intuitive Leadership.* Grand Rapids: Baker Books, 2007, 239-40.
[7] Henri Nouweni. *In the Name of Jesus: Reflections on Christian Leadership.* New York: The Crossroad Publishing Co., 1989.

liked, maybe even cool and popular, but it is imperative that Christian leaders, through prayer and accountability, resist this temptation.

Effective Christian leaders also resist the temptation to be spectacular. When leaders give into this temptation they begin to think of themselves as indispensable; as if their church would fall apart without them. In some cases this might actually happen, but this would only prove the ineffectiveness of that individual's leadership. I agree with the philosophy of North Point Ministries which says that effective leaders strategically replace themselves by preparing someone to do what they do.[8]

Finally, the ability to resist the temptation to be powerful also makes an effective Christian leader. In discussing this temptation, Nouwen writes, "One of the greatest ironies in the history of Christianity is that its leaders constantly gave in to the temptation of power… even though they continued to speak the name of Jesus, who did not cling to his divine power, but emptied himself and became as we are."[9] In discussing power and its relation to theology, knowledge and what kind of power Christians should exercise, Miroslav Volf suggests that this power, "is neither 'worldly power' nor 'no power' but 'the power of the crucified Christ.'"[10] Effective Christian leaders will not cling to their own worldly power, but rather they live in the power of Christ given to us through the Holy Spirit.

---

[8] Andy, Joiner & Jones, 2004, 158.
[9] Nouwen, p.58
[10] Miroslav Volf. *The Future of Theology: Essays in Honor of Jurgen Moltmann*. Grand Rapids: William B. Eerdmans Publishing, 1996, 109.

In the 21st century, effective church leaders need to be prepared to emphasize and demonstrate ethical leadership, personal responsibility, and community service. The foundation for success in all those areas lies in the ability of church leaders to initiate, develop, and maintain positive functioning relationships.

The call to be a church leader may take the form of preacher, pastor, teacher, counselor, missionary, small group leader, or other church related ministry, but no matter what the call, the Church needs to identify and provide leaders with the knowledge, skills, and abilities necessary to reach today's culture. Current church leaders need to prepare others for effective leadership by educating, equipping, enriching, and empowering them for the work of the Church in general, and life in the world at large.

In the 21st century the Church will need godly leaders capable of influencing others for a life of influence if it is to achieve its mission. Leaders must understand church government and politics, the effects of diversity in theology and worship, and the spiritual formation of church followers, program planning, and administration, as well as age-level specific best practices. Just as important, church leaders must be prepared to emphasize and demonstrate ethical leadership, personal responsibility, and community service through the initiation, development, and maintenance of positive functioning relationships.

Apart from the pastors, most churches normally have an administrative structure that supports church ministry. Some churches have the offices of Deacons and Elders. The functions of these offices vary from church to church. In Christ is the Answer Ministries which I am very familiar with, the Deacons are charged with the responsibility to oversee administrative functions, such as developing human resource policies, hiring and firing staff, etc. They are also in charge of Finance and administration. Elders on the other hand, are responsible for the spiritual well-being of the church. They develop and implement policies associated with church doctrine and emerging contemporary spiritual matters.

Church ministry usually involves teams of individuals who feel the burden for specific ministries. Some of the ministries in the church could be: Men's ministry, Women ministry, Youth ministry, Sunday School ministry, Widows and Widowers ministry, etc. It helps if each member of the team has a clear sense of calling and has the requisite character and commitment to serve. Bill Hybels in his book "Courageous Leadership" advances the view that while selecting people to serve on a team one should consider three non-negotiable qualities; namely character, competence and chemistry; in that order.

Christian Discipleship

Jesus came to save the world, and to that end he died, but on his way to the cross he concentrated his life on making a few disciples. These men were taught to do the same, until through the process of reproduction, the gospel of the kingdom would reach to the ends of the earth.[11] Over the ages the gospel has been preached through a variety of ways. The gospel is preached in church and in crusades. Other times it is through house to house evangelism. Through this variety of ways the objective is not just conversion of souls but making of disciples.

The mission given by Jesus to the disciples was to "go therefore and make disciples of all nations, baptizing them in the name of the Father and of the Son and of the Holy Spirit, and teaching them to obey everything that I have commanded you" (Matt 28:19–20a,). Their mission was not to save souls, which is God's business, but to make disciples of Jesus Christ who would then make disciples of Jesus Christ who would then make disciples of Jesus Christ, and so on. And what is a disciple of Jesus Christ? It is a person who imitates him. It is a person who does what Jesus did, reacts like Jesus did when he strode the earth in human form. Dallas Willard expresses it this way: "A disciple, or apprentice, is simply someone who has decided to be with another person, under appropriate conditions, in order to become capable of doing what that person does or to become what that person is."[12] In the Devotional Reading, Max Lucado expresses this reality by likening discipleship to seeking to have Jesus's heart.

---

[11] Leroy Eims. *The Lost Art of Disciple making*. Navpress. 1978, 9
[12] Dallas Willard, 1998. *The Divine Conspiracy: Rediscovering Our Hidden Life in God*. HarperSanFranscisco, 282.

The call of the Great Commission is not merely to make converts but to make disciples. The master plan for evangelism starts with converts, but does not end with it. The ultimate aim is for spiritual maturity. We must continually remind ourselves that disciplemaking begins with converts but does not end there. A large part of the New Testament is devoted to growing in Christ-likeness. Discipleship is the gradual, life-long process of growing closer to Jesus Christ in personal intimacy and becoming more like him.

To be a disciple means changing the way we live our everyday lives. What we do with our time. What we do with our money. With whom we spend our time. On whom and what we spend our money. We interact with time, money and people constantly. It is through them that we encourage our own discipleship and nurture the discipleship of others.

Edmund Chan who is the senior pastor of Covenant Evangelical Free Church in Singapore coined this philosophy of discipleship "It is all about a certain kind of person who is radically committed to a certain kind of purpose, who through a certain kind of process reproduces a certain kind of product."[13] He went further to define disciple making as "a process of bringing people into right relationship with God; and developing them to full maturity in Christ through intentional growth strategies, that they might multiply the entire process in others also."

---

[13] Edmund Chan. *Built to last – Towards a Disciple making Church*. (Covenant Resource Centre) 2001, 9

Nurturing spirituality involves a lifestyle of discipleship and evangelism, and these two processes reinforce each other. Discipleship is concerned with the post-conversion half of the spectrum of spirituality. Nurturing spirituality relates to a lifestyle of evangelism and discipleship. When we are part of the process of introducing people to Jesus and encouraging them to grow after they have come to know him, we discover that our own passion and spiritual vitality is enhanced. Few joys compare with the experience of seeing a friend come to new life in Christ. And one of life's deepest satisfactions is witnessing the gradual miracle of personal transformation in converts who are serious about becoming disciples.

Discipleship can be accomplished through a variety of approaches. In my few years of ministry I am persuaded that one of the primary ways is the consistent study of the Bible. The word intake can occur through listening to the word being preached in church or on radio. One can also read for themselves. In addition to reading it is more profitable to study and journal important lessons from the text. It is even much better to memorize some of the Bible verses that are particularly significant. The last approach is to meditate on the word which has come in via hearing, reading, study and memory. I have observed that anyone who regularly interacts with the word of God grows spiritually. This process just like River Nile is unstoppable. The intake of God's word works more like a human being taking in physical food. Once you put the food in the mouth, chew and swallow you never worry about what is happening inside your body. You know that once the food is inside of you, nourishment will occur naturally.

Every believer in Jesus Christ deserves the opportunity of personal nurture and development.[14] Every believer is expected to achieve his or her full potential for God. And most of them would if they had the opportunity, if someone would get the spiritual food within reach, if someone would give them the help they need, if someone would give them the training they should have, and if someone would care enough to suffer a little, sacrifice a little, and pray a lot. Spiritual growth is not instant. True growth takes time. On the leader's part, it takes the faith to see potential in the people as God expects them to be and wants them to become.

Another important discipline in discipleship is prayer. Primarily prayer is communication with God. Many people approach prayer as some kind of shopping list presented to God. Prayer is much more than asking God to do stuff for us. It is advisable during prayer to incorporate an aspect of adoration to God and confession of our sins. Such sins might be sins of omission or commission. Another important component is thanksgiving. This helps one reflect on what God has done before. The component of presenting our needs to God is called supplication or petition. It is important to present not just our needs but also the needs of others to God.

---

[14] Eims, 11

Spiritual maturity also comes as a result of fellowship with other believers. In Proverbs 27:17 we see that "as iron sharpens iron, so one man sharpens another." There is also a specific command for Christians not to neglect meeting together (Hebrews 10:25). Whereas it is important for Christians to congregate in a church setting, it is even more crucial to gather in small groups. The life of the church is really in the small groups that meet regularly, often in homes or cafes. Such small groups create conducive environments for one to feel safe enough to be vulnerable. There is nothing that I know that spurs spiritual growth as vulnerability.

In Christian community, we can open our lives to God's life by gathering regularly in small groups of two or more to encourage one another to discover the footprints of God in our daily existence and to venture out with God into areas where we have previously walked alone or not at all. But the aim is not external conformity, whether to doctrine or deed, but the re-formation of the inner self – of the spiritual core, the place of thought and feeling, of will and character.[15]

While the many Christian traditions differ over the details of spiritual maturity, they all come out at the same place: the transformation of the person into Christlikeness. Discipleship is the process of transforming the inner reality of the self (the inward being) in such a way that the overall life with God seen in the Bible naturally and freely comes to pass in us. Our inner world (the secret heart) becomes

---

[15] Lynda L. Graybeal and Julia L. Roller. *Connecting with God – A Spiritual Formation Guide*. Harper Collins eBooks. 2006

the home of Jesus, by his initiative and our response. As a result, our interior world becomes increasingly like the inner self of Jesus and, therefore, the natural source of words and deeds that are characteristic of him. By his enabling presence, we come to "let the same mind be in you that was in Christ Jesus" (Phil 2:5).

In order to spur holistic spiritual growth in the church it is necessary to espouse four kinds of engagement:[16]

1. Engaging with God (the life of worship and personal devotion).

2. Engaging with God's people (real *koinonia* through small groups and other means).

3. Engaging with your community (imaginative ways to distribute Christian witness through involvement in social needs — witness that is decentralized, grass roots, salt and light).

4. Engaging with the world (developing an awareness of and involvement in global mission).

The Church and State Relations

The church has got a critical role to play in the political life of the nation. According to New Testament writings the church is meant to be the salt and light of

---

[16] Mel Lawrenz. *Whole church: Leading from fragmentation to engagement*. Jossey-Bassa. 2009, p.11

the world (Matthew 5:13-14). The church acts as the moral conscience of the nation.[17] This means that the church leadership should guide the political systems for better governance. This emanates from the fact that the Gospel which the church preaches is holistic encompassing both the spiritual and the social dimension.[18] If the church loses sight of this prophetic mandate, it risks becoming irrelevant.

For some, Africa is synonymous with strife, hunger, corruption and lately human rights abuses (Adar & Munyae;[19] Gunda & Kügler[20]). For others, Africa is synonymous with rich resources, minerals, metals, fertile soils. Yet for others, Africa is synonymous with "rampant mass victimization", exploitation and plunders through slavery, colonialism, neo-colonialism, capitalism, and lately, despotism has reduced most Africans to victims.

The African Forum on Religion and Government (AFREG) noted that Africa is characterized by being the wealthiest continent in terms of natural resources and yet having the poorest people on planet earth.[21] It is known as incurably religious people and yet having a serious lack of authentic spirituality, morality and integrity in all aspects of life. They came to the conclusion that the African challenge is

---

[17] D.S. Parsitau. From Voices of the People to Discordant/Stifled Voices: Theological, Ethical and Social Political Voice and Voicelessness in a Multicultural/Religious Space, Perspectives from Kenya in Studia Historiae Ecclesiaticae(SHE) Journal of the Church History Society of Southern Africa, University of Pretoria, 2012, XXXV III

[18] D.S. Kioko. *The Response of the African Inland Church to Politics in Masinga District: 1975-2010 (Machakos County), Kenya*. Unpublished M.A. Thesis, Kenyatta University. 2013.

[19] Korwa D. Adar & Munyae, I.M. Human Rights Abuse in Kenya under Daniel Arap Moi, 1978-2001. *Africa Studies Quarterly*, 2001 Vol 5 Issue 1, 17pp

[20] M.R. Gunda & Kugler, J. (Ed.). *The Bible and Politics in Africa*. University of Bamberg Press. 2012.

[21] AFREG. *African Forum on Religion and Government*. International Leadership Foundation. 2006.

primarily one of leadership. During AFREG 1 which was held in Abuja, Nigeria in 25-28, July, 2006 the gathering of about 200 Christian women and men representing church and public sector leadership from 27 African countries and from the African Diaspora in the United States of America resolved to build a movement of African leaders of integrity who are committed to transforming Africa into a First World continent (a continent characterized by excellence) shaped by God-centred values.

This gathering expressed a sigh of hope given that a number of Christians are responding to the calling to be in active politics with the value of integrity, and the commitment to make a difference. This meeting came up with a number of commitments, such as calling upon African churches to commit themselves to encourage those who are called to engage in public politics and help in the building of their capacity to do so with the highest level of integrity as models to the entire society.

There are numerous moral and ethical challenges facing Kenya. Some of these include the run-away corruption, same sex marriages, whether or not to legalize abortion, whether or not to legalize commercial sex, among others. It would be naïve to assume that legislation is the only deterrent measure. However, proper legislation accompanied by law enforcement will go a long way in addressing some, if not, all of the moral and ethical concerns. Without the good will of the government and its agencies it will be difficult to address these social ills. Schluter observed that both in church history and today, a large part of Christian political involvement has focused on three areas of concern. These are issues of injustice and oppression, issues relating to the poor and weak in society, and issues concerned with the family.[22]

Several studies have been undertaken on the single issue of corruption (DFID;[23] Hoseah;[24] Kimeu;[25] Martini;[26] and Theron & Lotter).[27] Consequently, there are several publications to this effect. Some of these publications have addressed Kenya's corruption problem by examining causes and consequences. One publication even questions whether Kenya is on the right track when it comes to fighting corruption. Another publication focuses on Anti-corruption agencies and scrutinizes rhetoric versus reality. The Anglo-Leasing Corruption Scandal in Kenya has also captured the attention of many scholars. Stiftung in the Kenya Country Report stated that in the next few years, Kenya will face three principal challenges.[28] These are the full implementation of the fundamental devolution reform, the national

---

[22] M. Schluter. Christian strategy in the political arena. *Churchman: A Journal of Anglican Theology*. 1987, 334-343.

[23] DFID. *Why Corruption Matters: Understanding Causes, effects and how to address them*. Evidence aper on Corruption, 2015, January.

[24] E.G. Hoseah Corruption as a global hindrance to promoting ethics, integrity, and sustainable development in Tanzania: the role of the anti-corruption agency. *Journal of Global Ethics*. 2014, 10(3), 384-392.

[25] S. Kimeu. Corruption as a challenge to global ethics: the role of Transparency International. *Journal of Global Ethics,* 201410(2), 231-237.

[26] M. Martini. *Kenya: Overview of Corruption and Anti-Corruption*. Transparency International. 2012.

[27] P.M. Theron & Lotter, G.A. Corruption: How Should Christians Respond? *Acta Theologica* 201, 32(1), 96-117

[28] B. Stiftung. Kenya Country Report. 2016.

security crisis and the grand scale and endemic corruption. The first two years of the Uhuru Kenyatta government saw the loss of almost US$ 4 billion (KES 370 billion) due to corruption. This amount is equivalent to 22% of the Kenya's 2014/2015 budget.

This paper proposes that politics is one of the drivers of social transformation and hence the need for Christian leaders to actively participate in the political landscape of the nation. The focus of this paper is on social transformation as it relates to matters of social justice. Social justice is used in the restricted notion of a just society, where all people have adequate access to resources, opportunity and a say in decisions that affect their lives. Undoubtedly, most societies including Kenya experience inequality and exclusion. Social change attempts to reduce this inequality and exclusion.

Parsitau reported the changing roles of mainline churches in public life by exploring the perceived loss of prophetic voice on the part of the mainline church clergy and the emergence of other voices in the context of increased ethnicity and religious pluralism in multi-cultural space.[29]

Kwaka and others concluded that good leadership was the most critical factor if good governance can be realized in Kenya.[30] With each successive General

---

[29] Parsitau, 2012
[30] J. Kwaka, Okombo, O., Muluka, B., & Sungura-Nyabuto, B. (Ed.). *Challenging the rulers: A leadership model for good governance*. East African Educational Publishers. 2011.

election, Kenyans' collective hopes are raised that the incoming government will be accountable and facilitate holistic national development. A case in point is the 2002 General election which ushered in the NARC government whose campaign platform was zero tolerance to corruption. In 2003 the media reported that Kenyans were the most optimistic people in the world. However, it did not take long before the Anglo-leasing corruption scandal erupted. It would seem that every government since independence is characterized by a scandal.

Given the prevailing moral and ethical issues bedeviling Kenya, it is necessary to interrogate the role of the church in the political space. One is left wondering if it would make a difference if more Christian leaders offered themselves for elective office. Over the years a small number of Christian leaders have contested for political office. But as expected, an even smaller number gets elected. The perception by many is that the numbers of Christian leaders who join government are too few to make an impact on the social transformation of this country. There needs to be a debate as to the main role Christian leaders can play in politics to bring about a real and sustainable transformation. We need to clarify whether we are looking for Christian leaders in politics or any kind of leaders but who are transformational. It is quite possible that we can have transformative leaders who are not necessarily Christians.

Is it possible for the church to make a social impact outside of politics? What guarantee is there that if we have Christians occupying political office, then righteousness will abound in the land? Righteousness is being used here to refer to aspects of social justice and equity, not personal right standing with God through Jesus Christ. The assumption here is that Christian leaders who occupy elective office will seek to make a difference by staying the course, upholding high levels of integrity and embracing a transformative agenda. Further, we assume that such leaders will not compromise their Christian values and ethos.[31] If indeed Christians are the "salt and light of the world" it is necessary for them to stand up and be counted. The subject of political participation has been well researched. However, very little is reported regarding participation of Christian leaders in elective politics.

Religion may mean many things to different people. This paper will adopt a more narrow definition suggesting that religion has to do with the human experience of the sacred or transcendent. Since this paper is about the role of Christian leaders in the political space, we shall adopt a more narrow view and focus on the Christian religion. In fact, we shall be concerned with the evangelical perspective of the Christian religion.

The religious faith with the most number of adherents in Kenya is Christianity. It is estimated that Christians make up 82% of the entire population. The Christians fall into three broad categories, namely Catholics (23%), Protestants (47%), and

---

[31] AFREG, 2006

other Christians (12%) of the Kenyan population.

Religion can be seen on three fronts. Firstly, it acts as a medium of facilitating connectivity between humans and a higher deity. Secondly, it is a framework for morality and ethics that appeals to people's consciences. Thirdly, it contributes to provision of the infrastructure that facilitates human welfare and development.

Church and Politics

There are various approaches to church involvement in politics (Gitari;[32] Shiwati;[33] and Tarimo).[34] This may take the form of enthusiastic support, passive support, evaluative / critical engagement (constructive dialogue) and outright opposition. The approach followed by any church to the political dimension is informed to a great extent by the scope of the people's perceptions of religion in public life. If religion is limited to the private order of personal spirituality, then the church as a religious institution tends to steer away from public or political affairs. This is based on the dichotomy of the sacred vs. the secular. Indigenous African worldview was built on an integral whole without separation of the secular and the

---

[32] D.M. Gitari. *The Church's witness to the living God in seeking just political, social and economic structures in contemporary Africa*. (Eds.) Gitari D.M. & Benson, P. Africa Theological Fraternity. 1987.

[33] B. Shiwati. Church and politics in Africa Today: Validating African Christian Witness with special reference to Reconciliation as a Christian Principle. AICMAR Bulletin, an Evangelical Christian Journal of Contemporary Missions Outreach in Africa. 2008. Vol. 7

[34] A. Tarimo. Religion and Civil society: Challenges and Prospects for Eastern Africa. Journal of Hekima College. The Jesuit School of Theology. 2009.

sacred; (Smith[35] and Chepkwony.[36]) From the standpoint of biblical and theological teachings as well as the history of the church, religion and politics (Christianity and politics in particular) have been intimately related.

In Africa, the response of the church to political process has been witnessed in countries like South Africa, Nigeria, Ghana, Cameroon, Guinea, Uganda, Tanzania and even Kenya. Involvement of the church in politics has been achieved through ecumenical institutions and by individual church ministers. This participation has been in areas such as governance, violation of human rights, justice, apartheid, and democracy (Gitari;[37] Okullu;[38] Mugambi;[39] and Borer.[40])

There are basically three schools of thoughts on the involvement of Christians in politics.[41] On one extreme, sectarianism urges believers to isolate themselves completely from political process. On the other extreme, Christendom teaches that the church should seek to influence society for Christ from a position of political power. The balanced position states that Christians individually may be involved in

---

[35] D. Smith. *Religion, Politics and Social Change in the third world: A source book*: London Macmillan Publishers. 1971

[36] A.K. Chepkwony. *African Religion and Modern African States*, In: Gichure, I. & Benson, P. (Eds). Religion and Politics in Africa: Theological Reflections for the 21st Century. Nairobi. Pauline's Publication. 2008.

[37] Gitari, 1987

[38] H. Okullu. *Church and state in nation building and human development*. Nairobi: Uzima Press. 2003.

[39] J.N.K. Mugambi. *Church and State Relations: A Challenge for African Christianity*. Nairobi. Action Publishers. 2004.

[40] A.T. Borer. *Challenging the State: Churches as Political Actors in South Africa 1980-1994*. Notre Dame: University of Notre Dame Press. 1998.

[41] D. Cheddie. Should Christians Enter Politics? 2001

politics but the church as a body should abstain.

Some Christians believe that society is in its current state primarily because Christians have been complacent. This is subject to debate. It is naïve to presume that if our political leaders are "righteous" then that righteousness would be transferred to the general populace.

The notion of whether or not politics and religion should be kept apart is highly controversial in today's world. There is often talk of separation between church and state. Many Christians have approached politics as if it lies outside their primary realm of responsibilities. Politics are often viewed as part of the "world" that Christians ought not to love. Often times our Christian life becomes confined to personal godliness, to church activities, to attending liturgies, etc. We live in a world shaped by false post-Enlightenment divisions between private personal faith and public political life.

Kioko looked at the response of the Africa Inland Church (AIC) to politics in Masinga District in the Republic of Kenya.[42] The purpose of his study was to examine the response of AIC to Kenyan politics. This study aimed at investigating the factors affecting the apathy of AIC to politics from 1975-2010 and employed a descriptive research design and used purposive and simple random sampling

---
[42] Kioko, 2013

techniques for data collection and a theological framework for social ethics in discussing the response of the church to politics.

The study revealed that the factors underlying the response of any church to politics are not only limited to theological and doctrinal assumptions but also political, denominational, administrative structures and ethnocentrism. He concluded that AIC is one of the silent churches in Kenya in regard to politics. AIC does not involve herself in political issues unless they directly affect her moral and spiritual values. Further, he noted that AIC concentrates on spiritual perspectives, an aspect borrowed from the founding mission AIM. The non involvement in the socio-political welfare of the people leads to betrayal of the holistic nature of the Gospel as well as loss of relevance of the church.

It is widely assumed by many biblical scholars in Europe that the era of a Bible-influenced politics is gone, much in the same way that some scholars would argue that the role of religion in the public sphere has waned since the 1970s as Europe secularized herself.

In Kenya, the participation of the church in politics can be traced from the colonial period. According to Haynes[43] and Githiga,[44] the relationship between the church and state during the colonial era was that of a joint hegemony. However, at

---

[43] J. Haynes. *Religion and Politics in Africa.* Nairobi. East African Educational Publishers. 1996.
[44] G.G. Githiga. *The Church as the bulwark against authoritarianism: Development of Church and State Relations in Kenya with particular reference to the years after political independence 1963-1992.* Regnum. 2001, pp217

times this relationship was faced with certain disagreements over policy issues. The missionary church shared power with the colonial administration as the key missionaries were incorporated in the Legislative Council (Legco). In this arrangement, the missionary church did not speak against the authoritarianism of the colonial government.

In independent Kenya, church involvement in political processes was predominantly through the Catholic Church, the Anglican Church and the National Council of Churches of Kenya (NCCK) and its member churches. Notable church ministers due to their prophetic voice include the late Alexander Muge, the late Henry Okullu, the late David Gitari, the late Manasses Kuria, Timothy Njoya, and Ndingi Mwana-a-Nzeki. Their contribution to the political process was through the quest for right governance, against violation of human rights, against electoral procedures, constitutional reforms, and against negative ethnicity. Parsitau has reported the rise to public prominence of the Pentecostal and charismatic movements as key elements within civil society in the governance of the state in Kenya.[45]

It is noteworthy, that it was not just the clergy who spoke against the misdeeds of the government. There were a number of prominent politicians such as

---

[45] D.S. Parsitau. From the Fringes to the Centre: Rethinking the role of religion in public sphere in Kenya. Council for the Development of Social Science Research in Africa (CODESRIA) 12th *General Assembly* 07-11/12/2008, Younde Cameroon.

the late George Anyona, Koigi wa Wamwere, Mwashengu wa Mwachofi, Abuya Abuya, the late Martin Shikuku, James Orengo, the late Jean-Marie Seroney, the late Chelagat Mutai, Mwandawiro Mganga, Lawrence Sifuna, Chibule wa Tsuma, among others. Adar and Munyae (2001) give a detailed chronology of some of the human rights abuses that predominated President Moi's reign (1978-2001). It all started with the institutionalization, centralization and personalization of the presidency. This was followed closely by assassination, repression and detention without trial of dissidents.

It should be noted, however, that these human rights abuses did not start with the Moi regime. Jomo Kenyatta's reign was littered with such malpractices as the Wagalla massacre, the mass shootout in Kisumu in 1969, the assassination of Tom Mboya, Pio Gama Pinto and J.M. Kariuki, among others. It is regrettable that these human rights abuses continued unabated even when Kenya returned to the multiparty democracy in the 1990's.

The question as to whether churches and other houses of worship should keep out of political matters or whether they should express their views on day-to-day social and political questions has lingered over the ages. For example Himes reported that for more than a decade a clear majority of those who were polled answered that the churches should express their views on social and political questions.[46] However, as recently as 2012, 54% of respondents thought the churches should keep out of political matters. There is uncertainty as to why the shift occurred in public attitude about the role of the churches in political affairs.

The bane of leadership whether in Church or the wider society is the whole question of trust. In fact, the more appropriate way of putting it is that we have a trust-deficit in our society. David Horsager (2021) through research developed what he terms the 8 pillars of trust that drive results.

Clarity: *People trust the clear and mistrust or distrust the ambiguous.* Be clear about your mission, purpose, expectations, and daily activities. When we are clear about priorities on a daily basis, we become productive and effective. Servant-leaders rely on persuasion, rather than positional authority in making decisions. Servant-leaders seek to convince others, rather than coerce compliance. This particular element offers one of the clearest distinctions between the traditional authoritarian model and that of servant-leadership. The servant-leader is effective at building consensus within groups.

Clarity is most often demonstrated in what and how we communicate. We communicate verbally and non-verbally. We communicate written values about us and about the organizations we lead. We also communicate unwritten values. Most importantly, what we say needs to align with what we do. One of the critical roles of

---

[46] K.R. Himes. *Christianity and the Political order*. In Phan, P.C. (Ed.) Theology in Global Perspective Series (pp. 1-17). Maryknoll, New York: Orbis Books, 2013.

a leader is to rally people around a particular vision. It is very important that the rallying call be as clear as is humanly possible. The followers should have no doubts as to the direction the organization is going. And consequently, the followers will own the vision and be accountable for the success of the organization.

Compassion: *People put faith in those who care beyond themselves.* People are often skeptical about whether someone really has their best interests in mind. "Do unto others as you would have them do unto you" is not just an old saying. It is a bottom-line truth. Follow it, and you will build trust. Servant-leaders strive to understand and empathize with others. People need to be accepted and recognized for their special and unique spirit. One must assume the good intentions of coworkers and not reject them as people, even when forced to reject their behavior or performance.

A leader who demonstrates compassion toward the followers creates an environment for the followers to be loyal to the cause. The followers often go the extra mile while serving under a compassionate leader. Most followers detest the notion that they are just a statistic. They need to feel that their dignity is valued. It doesn't matter whether the follower is a junior staff or a senior staff. Each person contributes to the growth of the organization. A compassionate leader will help bring down the class divide that is often prevalent in many organizations.

Character: *People notice those who do what is right ahead of what is easy.* Leaders who have built this pillar consistently do what needs to be done when it needs to be done, whether they feel like doing it or not. It is the work of life to do what is right rather than what is easy. This pillar speaks of authenticity. Any leader worth his or her salt must demonstrate fidelity of character. Leaders who are true to themselves are not swayed by every opinion. Such leaders say what needs to said without the fear of possible repercussions. A leader of character will be willing to risk his / her comfort or interests for the sake of the organization. Character also has to do with integrity. Many leaders fail on this account. Some get caught up in compromising situations. Others are entangled in shady deals where there is a clear conflict of interest. Some others engage in corrupt practices which feed into their own greed. Followers find it relatively easy to follow leaders of character.

Competency: *People have confidence in those who stay fresh, relevant, and capable.* The humble and teachable person keeps learning new ways of doing things and stays current on ideas and trends. Make a habit of reading, learning, and listening to fresh information. Life is a school where we never graduate. Each new day offers us an opportunity to learn a new thing. It is incumbent upon every leader to strive to competent in what they do. This competence is very attractive to followers. The Bible reminds us that King David shepherded Israel with integrity of heart and with skillful hands (Psalm 78:72). Leaders ought to prioritize continuous learning. Today's challenges cannot be solved by yesterday's knowledge. The leader must continually sharpen the axe of leadership.

Commitment: *People believe in those who stand through adversity.* People trusted General Patton, Martin Luther King, Jr., Mohandas Gandhi, Jesus, and George Washington because they saw commitment and sacrifice for the greater good. Commitment builds trust. Leaders who demonstrate commitment draw many followers. Commitment on the part of the leader demonstrates fidelity to the cause. It proves beyond doubt the clear focus with which the leader's eye is trained on the vision and goals of the organization. Followers find it easy to follow leaders who articulate clearly where they are going. Servant-leaders believe that people have an intrinsic value beyond their tangible contributions as workers. As such, servant-leaders are deeply committed to a personal, professional, and spiritual growth of each and every individual within the organization.

Notable church ministers due to their prophetic voice include the late Alexander Muge, the late Henry Okullu, the late David Gitari, the late Manasses Kuria, Timothy Njoya, and Ndingi Mwana-a-Nzeki. Their contribution to the political process was through the quest for right governance, against violation of human rights, against electoral procedures, constitutional reforms, and against negative ethnicity. Many of them paid the ultimate price. They left a legacy worth emulating.

Connection: *People want to follow, buy from, and be around those who are willing to connect and collaborate.* Trust is all about relationships, and relationships are best built by establishing genuine connection. Develop the trait of gratitude, and you will be a magnet. The late Dr. Gary Smalley is known to have stated that "life is all about relationships, the rest is details." Relationships must be nurtured. It takes time and effort to nurture relationships. Relationships are sometimes messy especially in cases of conflict. Some relationships are dysfunctional and require devotion to mend them. A leader must consciously prioritize relationships. Theodore Roosevelt stated that "People don't care how much you know until they know how much you care."

Contribution: *Few things build trust quicker than actual results.* At the end of the day, people need to see outcomes. You can have compassion and character, but without the results you promised, people won't trust you. Be a contributor who delivers real results. It is a human phenomenon that people prefer to align with success stories. In a sense people are attracted to a moving bus. Especially one that is moving in the right direction.

Consistency: *It's the little things—done consistently—that make the biggest difference.* If I am overweight, it is because I have eaten too many calories over time, not because I ate too much yesterday. It is the same in business. The little things done consistently make for a higher level of trust and better results. The power of discipline and habit is best displayed in consistency. Many leaders expect the miraculous. In as much as God still performs miracles, it takes the painstaking discipline of doing something consistently in order to produce lasting results. Anything worth celebrating does not come via lottery but through hard work, discipline and the sweat of the brow.

Conclusion

This publication discusses the critical significance of servant leadership in the Church and society. The author advances the position that leadership in church should emulate the model set by Jesus Christ himself. The paper begins with a brief definition of leadership and the functions of leadership. Then the author zeroes in on servant leadership and characteristics of effective Christian leaders. Christian discipleship is then discussed followed by church – state relations and church and politics. The author posits that leadership and church ministry ought to engage with the society for impact. Church ministry does not happen in a vacuum. It is incumbent upon the church to engage with the context for societal transformation. Finally, the author highlights the critical place trust plays in the life of a leader. Trust-deficit is one of the reasons many organizations, churches, and nations fail. Leaders must cultivate clarity and compassion in their leadership. The leader should demonstrate good character, competency, commitment, connection in order to make a contribution to society. All these attributes can only be achieved through consistency which many leaders consider too high a price to pay. Everything in life costs something.

Bibliography

Adar, G.K. & Munyae, I.M. (2001). Human Rights Abuse in Kenya under Daniel Arap Moi, 1978-2001. *African Studies Quarterly* Vol5 Issue 1.

AFREG, (2006). *African Forum on Religion and Government*. International Leadership Foundation.

Borer, A.T. (1998). *Challenging the State: Churches as Political Actors in South Africa 1980-1994*. Notre Dame: University of Notre Dame Press.

Chan, Edmund. 2001. *Built to last – Towards a Disciple making Church*. (Covenant Resource Centre).

Cheddie, D. (2001). Should Christians Enter Politics? http://www.bibleissues.org/politics1.html

Chepkwony, A.K. (2008). *African Religion and Modern African States*, In: Gichure, I. & Benson, P. (Eds) Religion and Politics in Africa: Theological Reflections for the 21st Century. Nairobi. Pauline's Publication.

Clinton, J. Robert.1988. *The making of a leader*.Navpress.

Coleman, Robert E. 1993. *The Master Plan of Evangelism*. Fleming H. Revell.

DFID (2015). *Why Corruption Matters: Understanding Causes, effects and how to address them*. Evidence Paper on Corruption.

Eims, Leroy. 1978. *The Lost Art of Disciple making*. Navpress.

Gitari, D. M. (1987). *The Church's witness to the living God in seeking just political, social and economic structures in contemporary Africa*. (Eds.). Gitari D. M. & Benson, P., Africa Theological Fraternity.

Githiga, G.G. (2001). *The Church as the Bulwark Against Authoritarianism: Development of Church and State Relations in Kenya with Particular Reference to the Years After Political Independence 1963-1992*. Regnum.

Grahn, Thorsten. 2011. The Three Sisters Garden Analogy for Servant Leadership Based Collaboration. *The Journal of Virtues & Leadership*, Vol.2 Iss.1, Summer.

Graybeal, Lynda L.l and Julia L. Roller. 2006. *Connecting with God – A Spiritual Formation Guide*. Harper Collins eBooks.

Greenleaf, Robert K. 1977. *Servant Leadership: a journey into the nature of legitimate power and greatness*. Paulistic Press: New Jersey.

Gunda M.R. & Kügler, J., (Ed.). (2012). *The Bible and Politics in Africa*. University of Bamberg Press.

Haynes, J. (1996). *Religion and Politics in Africa*. Nairobi. East African Educational Publishers.

Himes, K.R. (2013). *Christianity and the Political Order*. In Phan, P.C. (Ed.),

Theology in Global Perspective Series (pp. 1-17). Maryknoll, New York: Orbis Books

Horsager, David. (2021). Trusted Leader: 8 Pillars That Drive Results. Berrett Koehler Publishers.

Hoseah, E. G.(2014). Corruption as a global hindrance to promoting ethics, integrity, and sustainable development in Tanzania: the role of the anti-corruption agency. *Journal of Global Ethics*, *10*(3), 384–392. https://doi.org/10.1080/17449626.2014.973995

Keel, Tim.2007. *Intuitive Leadership.* Grand Rapids: Baker Books.

Kimeu, S. (2014). Corruption as a challenge to global ethics: the role of Transparency International. *Journal of Global Ethics*, *10*(2), 231–237. https://doi.org/10.1080/17449626.2014.935982

Kioko, D.S. (2013). *The Response of the African Inland Church to Politics in Masinga District: 1975-2010 (Machakos County), Kenya.* Unpublished M.A. Thesis, Kenyatta University.

Kwaka, J., Okombo, O., Muluka, B., & Sungura-Nyabuto, B. (Ed.). (2011). *Challenging the Rulers: A Leadership Model for Good Governance.* East African Educational Publishers

Lawrenz, Mel. 2009. *Whole church: Leading from fragmentation to engagement.* Jossey-Bass.

Martini, M. (2012). *Kenya: Overview of Corruption and Anti-Corruption.* Transparency International.

Maxwell, John C.1998. *The 21 Irrefutable Laws of Leadership: Follow them and people will follow you*, Harper Collins Leadership.

Mugambi, J.N.K. (2004). *Church and State Relations: A Challenge for African Christianity.* Nairobi. Acton Publishers.

Nouweni, Henri.1989. *In the Name of Jesus: Reflections on Christian Leadership.* New York: The Crossroad Publishing Co.

Okullu, H. (2003). *Church and State in nation building and human development.* Nairobi: Uzima Press.

Oparanya, W. A. (2010). 2009 Population & Housing Census Results. GoK.

Parsitau, D. S. (2008). From the Fringes to the Centre: Rethinking the Role of Religion in the Public Sphere in Kenya. Council for the Development of Social Science Research in Africa (CODESRIA) 12th *General Assembly* 07-11/12/2008, Younde Cameroon.

Parsitau, D.S (2012) From Voices of the People to Discordant/Stifled Voices: Theological, Ethical and Social Political Voice and Voicelessness in a

Multicultural/Religious Space, Perspectives from Kenya in Studia Historiae Ecclesiaticae(SHE) Journal of the Church History Society of Southern Africa, University of Pretoria, XXXV 111

Schluter, M. (1987). Christian strategy in the political arena. *Churchman: A Journal of Anglican Theology*.

Shiwati, B. (2008). Church and Politics in Africa Today: Validating African Christian Witness with Special Reference to Reconciliation as a Christian Principle. AICMAR Bulletin, an Evangelical Christian Journal of Contemporary Missions Outreach in Africa Vol.7.

Smith, D. (1971). *Religion, Politics and Social Change in the third World: A source book*:London Macmillan Publishers.

Stanley Andy Reggie Joiner, and Lane Jones.2004. *7 Practices of Effective Ministry*. Colorado Springs: Multnomah Books.

Stiftung, B. (2016). Kenya Country Report.

Tarimo, A. (2009). Religion and Civil Society: Challenges and Prospects for Eastern Africa. *Journal of Hekima College*, The Jesuit School of Theology.

Theron, P. M., & Lotter, G. A. (2012). Corruption : How Should Christians Respond? *Acta Theologica 32*(1).

Volf, Miroslav. 1996. *The Future of Theology: Essays in Honor of Jurgen Moltmann*. Grand Rapids: William B. Eerdmans Publishing.

Willard, Dallas.1998. *The Divine Conspiracy: Rediscovering Our Hidden Life in God*. HarperSanFranscisco.

Contents

Introduction 2
Leadership functions... 4
Servant Leadership 5
Effective Christian Leaders 9
Christian Discipleship... 14
The Church and State Relations 20
Church and Politics... 27
Conclusion 39
Bibliography 40

I want morebooks!

Buy your books fast and straightforward online - at one of world's fastest growing online book stores! Environmentally sound due to Print-on-Demand technologies.

Buy your books online at
www.morebooks.shop

Kaufen Sie Ihre Bücher schnell und unkompliziert online – auf einer der am schnellsten wachsenden Buchhandelsplattformen weltweit! Dank Print-On-Demand umwelt- und ressourcenschonend produziert.

Bücher schneller online kaufen
www.morebooks.shop

info@omniscriptum.com
www.omniscriptum.com

OMNIScriptum

Milton Keynes UK
Ingram Content Group UK Ltd.
UKHW041951291124
451915UK00001B/128